Dedicated To All Of Those
Who Contribute To My Crazy...

**And A Very Special Thanks
To Those Who Tolerate It.**

But to be specific...Kelly Birkmaier (Mom), Neal Bergman (Dad), Nick Bergman (Brother), Stacey Campbell, Rob Oldham, Aileen Tormon, Michael Schur, Emily Jackson, Greg Gauthreaux, Robin Schroffel, Evelyn Keolian, Anna Tsurkis, Stella Papadopoulos, Adam Day, Kevin Wineinger, MJ Sagan and Derek Arnold as well as every family member, friend, girlfriend, roommate and coworker that I've ever had.

CRITICALLY ACCLAIMED!!!

"I accidentally used it as kindling for my fireplace. Worked well. Easy to tear. Flammable."
- Harold from Poughkeepsie

"This book drives me crazy."
- Carl from Sacramento

"Mom, Billy keeps punching me and then he farted."
- Young girl with Mom and Billy from Tulsa

"Wait. Is this one of those dopey self-help books about how life is crazy and you can't take it anymore?"
- Suzy from Chattanooga

"I'm a Nigerian prince in urgent need of transferring lottery winnings out of my country and away from the corrupt government. Please send me your bank account information."
- Prince from Nigeria (via email)

tit

If you do THIS...

I'll do THAT.
I'll definitely do THAT.
With vigor.
And enthusiasm.

for tat

you
drive
me

CrAZY!

Off We Go...

We all have those things in life that drive us up the wall, right? And not just a little up the wall. But seriously pull-your-hair-out-scream-at-that-top-of-your-lungs-kinda up the wall crazy. Things at home, work or elsewhere. With family members, spouses, friends, coworkers, strangers. With those that we're romantic with and those that we wish we weren't. Or had never been. And maybe we're even driven up the wall by ourselves. No! Not ourselves?! Well, maybe. Maybe even ourselves. Maybe especially ourselves. This is what has inspired this book.

Most recommended solutions to these irritating situations include a combination of communication, compassion and compromise. This book takes the opposite approach by fanning the flames of frustration a little higher. Letting the wheels come off. Letting all hell break loose. And then, the absurdity rushes in.

Doesn't that seem like more fun sometimes? Who's to say we can't pick at the scab of serenity every once in a while? Especially in a fun, light-hearted way that takes into account the multiple points of view of the family members, spouses and friends mentioned above. Because we're all guilty of annoying and being unnecessarily annoyed by each other? So try this at home*. At work*. And elsewhere*. Enjoy.

Now, let's get this boat a ROCKIN!!!

* Just kidding. Don't try this. I can't afford that kind of liability.

If you take bike-to-work week to mean that you can SHOW UP SWEATY to every morning meeting…

I'll suggest we hire locker room staff to SHAMMY you off as you arrive to the office.

If you invent a new series of all-office acronyms for E.V.E.R.Y.T.H.I.N.G. I.M.A.G.I.N.A.B.L.E.

I'll employ a language that goes along with it. B.I.W.D.K.W.A.O.T.N.A.M.W.M.A.W.H.F.W.I.R? (Because if we don't know what any of these new acronyms means we might as well have fun with it, right?)

If you propose another POINTLESS OFFICE POLICY like "timed bathroom breaks"…

I'll add a PIT STOP CHART in the hallway to document what we did while we were in there. 9:37am. 6oz pee. Lemon Daisy color. 27 seconds. Rinsed hands, but no soap.

If you litter your desk with more cups and candy wrappers than a TORNADO through DixieCupSnickersville...

I'll pass along FEMA's hotline information in hopes that it leads to you cleaning up your DISASTER ZONE.
1-800-I-Need-A-Bulldozer-And-A-Dumpster

If you take stuff from my desk WITHOUT ASKING...

I'll stop by your desk to ask for it back while sipping coffee from YOUR FAVORITE MUG. It's the one that says "Theft Police", right? With the big gold star?

If you HOVER over my desk to see what's on my computer monitor…

I'll anonymously send you email from an IMAGINARY OFFICE SECURITY DRONE (NSA@office.drone.com). Including photos of you looking around before clicking on a Buzzfeed link. Yeah, a NSFW one.

If you DECORATE YOUR HALF OF THE CUBICLE with a thousand photos of your beloved pet cat...

I'll CONVERT MY HALF into a Feng Shui shrine. No shoes please.

If you SMACK, SNAP AND POP
your bubble gum...

I'll SNIP, CLIP, AND FILE my nails
at my desk. All of them.
Toes included.

If you SNIFFLE SNIFFLE SNIFFLE
all day next to me...

I'll AHEM AHEM AHEM in your direction until you
get the hint to pick up a tissue.

If you constantly CLICK CLICK CLICK
your pen while you're thinking...

I'll do that weird leg BOUNCE BOUNCE
BOUNCY thing while I'm waiting
for you to make up your mind.

If you gossip more than TMZ…

I'll post your working-for-the-weekend Twitter account to the office bulletin board. Remind me again if it's work appropiate?

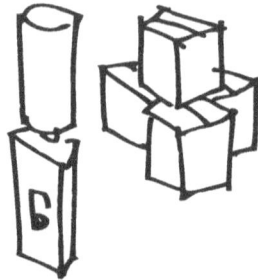

If YOU VOLUNTEER ME for the highway trash pickup that no one else wants to do...

I'll suggest that YOU ASSIST the moving-those-boxes-of-who-knows-what-to-storage committee. Yeah, the heavy ones behind the water cooler.

If you badger me into joining the GROUP SING-A-LONG for Larry from Accounting's 34th birthday...

I'll add THREE EXTRA CANDLES to your cake when it comes to your 38th...Er, I mean 41st.

If you refuse to turn your *CELL PHONE RINGER* off during our *must-get-stuff-done meetings...*

I'll blare CHRISTMAS MUSIC next to your desk every morning after Labor Day.

If you WASTE HALF OF OUR MEETING fumbling with the presentation set up...

I'll derail the rest of our time together with MY AWKWARD SOAP OPERA DRAMA story from last weekend. It's a long one. Kind of an epic three-part saga. One-part Leprechaun outfits. Another part in search of the pot of gold. With a grand finale of green drinks and regret.

If you send me to another meeting with NO SENSE OF PURPOSE...

I'll REPORT BACK a story about how fun I wish the meeting would've been. With unicorns, lasers and a tray of enticing-but-raisin-riddled cookies. Yum Yum TTZZZ Magic!!!

If you show up to all of our meetings HALF AN HOUR LATE...

I'll prepare us all for next get together by ALLOCATING TIME for your tardiness in the MEETING AGENDA:
1. *Jim arrives late. Apologizes with a joke about a monkey with a receding hairline. (32 min)*
2. *Peggy then vents her frustrations for more time wasted and hints about quitting. (3 min)*
3. *We all console each other and agree to be more punctual. (8 min)*

If you EAT your lunch while you're on the phone with me...

I'll make sure that you're on speakerphone so that we can make a GAME OF GUESSING what you're eating:

> *"Sounds like salt n' vinegar chips to me. Ruffles I think."*

> *"Doesn't sound that crunchy to me. Are you sure it's not really crispy bacon?"*

> *"Wait. I hear something sorta squishy too."*

If you blab on a PERSONAL PHONE CALL loud enough to make the entire office feel awkward about your newfound ailment...

I'll chime in with an UNSOLICITED DIAGNOSIS based upon your SYMPTOMS:

Fatigue + upset stomach = More salad and less burrito gut bombs for lunch.

If you send me 10 vague one-sentence emails...

I'll respond with a LONG-WINDED GABBY BLABBING MOTORMOUTHED voicemail with NO ACTUAL SUBSTANCE.

If you're always a TELEPHONE TOUGH GUY...

I'll take your cue and PLAY ALONG like we're in the midst of a WWII action movie scene. "We need more ammo, Charlie!" "Stanley, there's no ammo! There's only grit, sweat and the will to survive!"

If you use that tacky WESTERN-THEMED font for your emails one more time...

I'll tell the client that you're the world's BIGGEST LINE DANCE FAN and that you can't wait to shake a leg.

If you #TEXT with #MORE #CAPITALIZATION, #ABBREVIATION, #PUNCTUATION and #HASHTAGS than actual words?!?!?!?!?!?!?!?!? !?!?!?!?!?!?!?!?!?!?!?!?!?!?!?!?!?!?!?

I'll try to BALANCE OUT THE LITERARY WORLD by responding with the punctutional opposite: "capital t thanks for your message comma capital c carl exclamation point exclamation point any of the donuts leftover from your meeting question mark hashtag custard filled deliciousness get in my belly"

#?!?!

If you email me using a COMIC Sans font...

You're just kidding, right?
Because I read it like
"HAHAHA When can I expect those
HAHAHA expense reports? LOLOLOLOL!!!"

:) :) :) :) :)
:) :) :) :) :) :)

If you load your email messages with EMOJIS and motivational quotes about "being the better you"...

I'll join in the graphic inspirational-ness by adding you to the MAILING LIST of as many horoscopes and Zen flyers as I can find. You're a Sagitarrius I think?

If you TAKE CREDIT for every scrap of my work...

I'll point out every inkling of a FLAW in yours, you'res, and, of course, you ares.

whoopie!

If your INFLATED EGO overwhelms every room you walk into...

I'll WHOOPIE CUSHION your world until it's DEFLATED back to reality.

If you're always the FIRST TO CHIME IN with critiques of what I'm doing...

I'll always be the LAST TO FOLLOW THROUGH with whatever you suggest. (So passive aggressive...I know!)

If you STEAL MY THUNDER as I'm sharing my good news...

I'll RAIN ON YOUR PARADE when you're telling us about your new idea. Chance of precipitation=100%

If you reset the THERMOSTAT to 64 degrees again...

I'll wander around in a SCARF and PARKA asking if we can huddle together for warmth.

If you UNEXPECTEDLY RESTART the server as I'm trying to save the last four hours of work that I just finished for tomorrow's client presentation...

I'll OPEN EVERY SUSPECT email and its accompanying *.exe file. Oops.

If you ignore the PAPER JAM in the printer one more time...

I'll refill it with TACKY BORDERED PAPER once it's fixed. Yeah, the rainbow birthday one.

If you restock the vending machines with MULTIGRAIN this and RICE CAKE that...

I'll start a side business selling TWIX and SNICKERS from my desk. Because that's what we all want anyway.

If you SWAP my awesome new comfy chair for
your old one that creaks with every twist and turn...

**I'll SWITCH out your keyboard to one that
makes stupid dog toy sounds with every
keystroke. Squeaky. Squeaky.**

If you PAINT your fingernails at your desk again…

I'll AIR OUT my sweaty, smelly feet at mine.

**If you wear TOO MANY DOSES of cologne
again today...**

*I'll have BEANS and BROCCOLI for dinner tonight.
Because we all know what that means for tomorrow.*

when's lunch?

If you make us all hungry by yammering on at 10am with "WHEN'S LUNCH?"…

I'll tide myself over with a MID-MORNING SNACK of the Sandwich in the Refrigerator With Your Name Clearly Marked on It. Mmm. Such a tasty sandwich named Bill.

**If you switch the office's
turbocharged coffee to DECAF...**

*I'll treat it like PROHIBITION and set up
a BOOTLEG OPERATION out of the supply
closet to meet our caffeine needs.*

If you continually leave the sink FULL of dirty dishes...

**I'll assume that they're LEFTOVERS you're
in the midst of saving...of which I'll Zip-Lock
bag, tag, and place those tasty plates on your
desk for another time.**

**If you leave the coffee pot EMPTY every time
you leave the kitchen...**

*I'll assume that you missed Monotone Bob's
EQUIPMENT TRAINING SEMINAR and I'll sign you up
to learn how-to all over again. And again. And again.*

If you get less work done than the REALITY SHOW STARS you've been blabbing about all day...

I'll suggest we bring in a film crew to document your "productivity" tomorrow. LIGHTS! CAMERA! ACT busy!

If you PERSONAL TEXT MESSAGE your way through the entire workday...

I'll SUGGEST that you chip in on the company's data plan. Because I know you're stealing the just-for-work Wi-Fi too.

If you CALL IN "SICK" on the day before our deadline...

I'll ask EVERYONE ON THE OFFICE to phone you to make sure that you're "OK."
Ok? Ok? Ok? Ok? Ok? Ok? Ok? Ok? Ok?
Ok? Ok? Ok? Ok? Ok? Ok? Ok? Ok? Ok?
Ok? Ok? Ok? Ok? Ok? Ok? Ok? Ok? Ok?

If you ask again
HOW MUCH I MAKE...

I'll act like my bonus was big enough to pay for my entire family's HAWAIIAN VACATION.

you
drive
me

CrAZy!

at home

If you SNEEZE on my toothbrush...

I'll fart in the bathroom WHILE YOU'RE SHOWERING.

*If you demand that the TOILET PAPER
be installed on the holder a certain way...*

**I'll spell OCD in pee at the base
of the toilet.
Drip. Drip.
Dribble.**

*If you complain about HOW MUCH toilet paper
I use (because it's so so expensive)...*

**I'll only leave ONE SCRAP OF PAPER on the roll
every time I leave the seat. You know...to save
you from the temptation of using more than your
allotted quota.**

*If you want to argue about whether the
toilet seat is UP or DOWN again...*

**I'll neglect to WASH MY HANDS
every time that I use it. Wanna hug?**

*If you text me every minute with "just one more thing"
to get at the GROCERY STORE...*

**I will substitute your requests for diet-this and lite-
that...WITH BACON AND CHEESY CHEESY PUFFS.**

**If you drive us to 15+ DIFFERENT
shops to find your perfect
football sweater...**

*I'll force us all an EXTRA 30 miles to save
two cents on gas.*

*If you ask me to SKIP OUT on yoga in favor of
cleaning out the garage…*

**I'll ask you to STAND IN LINE at the post
office on the first summer Saturday. Oh.
And don't forget the stamps with the 4th of
July fireworks on them. Yeah, the
blue and red ones.**

If you sign me up as the CHAPERONE and SHUTTLE for the kids' upcoming school trip...

I'll feed them a breakfast of GUMMY BEARS and TOOTSIE ROLLS so that they're revved up for your bring-the-kids-to-work day.

If you mess up the *HIGHLY-ANTICIPATED* video recording of the kids' school play...

I'll save the day by dressing them as PIRATES and PRINCESSES for our next family photo. ARRRR!

If you give in to the kids' WHINING for ICE CREAM AND CAKE FOR DINNER again...

I'll throw a TEMPER TANTRUM every time they don't eat their vegetables.

If you CRITICIZE MY get-the-kids-to-do-their-homework technique...

I'll RATE YOUR storytelling skills to them. "B+ Could use more enthusiasm when saying 'Happy Hippopotamus' and 'Dancing Alligators.'"

If you let the kids watch SCARY MOVIES at night...

I'll BURST IN LIKE THE BOOGEYMAN as you're trying to put them to bed. Booga Booga BOO!!!

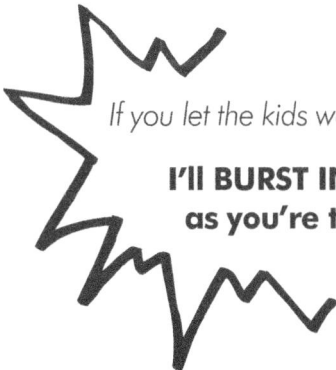

If you make the next dinner party's MAIN COURSE taste like a combination of muesli and Malt O' Meal...

I'll make brownies for DESSERT with cat food as the main ingredient. Mmmm...MOEWNIES. Makes my belly purrrrrr with delight.

meow

If you let our kitchen counter become a MOLDY OLD STAND of long-past-its-prime fruit...

I'll return the ORANGE JUICE CONTAINER back to the refrigerator with barely a drop left inside.

If you STINK UP the kitchen with burnt popcorn...

I'll smoke cigars in the living room to COMMEMORATE THE SCENT.

hay! ...is for horses

If you force me onto the same ALL-VEGGIE DIET you happen to be on...

I will SUGARY STOCK the kitchen cupboards with Cheetos and Double Stuf Oreos.

If you MISMATCH MY SOCKS while you're folding laundry one more time...

I'll replace your T-shirts and underwear with ones ONE SIZE TOO SMALL.

If you FORGET to take the dog out on the night that I have to work late...

I'll IGNORE the sink full of dirty dishes on the night before your parents come visit. Woof.

If you stack one more thing atop the trash bin like it's a game of JENGA...

I'll HOPSCOTCH around the imminent mess it'll make. And until you've cleaned it up.

If you PRETEND for six months like you'll fix the leaky kitchen sink ...

I'll only ACT like I'm going to bake your favorite cake for your birthday.

If you get jealous whenever another attractive woman is nearby...

I'll suggest you to DRESS UP as Halle Berry for our next bedroom escapades. Obviously in her Catwoman outfit. Puuurrrr-ROAR!!!

If you talk about our amazing vacation adventure like it was another HO-HUM week away...

I'll OVERSENSATIONALIZE my trip to the grocery store to sound like it was the best time ever. Because you know Rob Lowe was there. And so was Cher.

If you act like a little PUBLIC DISPLAY OF AFFECTION is the most awkward moment ever faced by mankind...

I'll bless you with the dopiest pet name ever bestowed upon the world, SCHMOOPY POOKEMS.

games
games
games!

apps
apps
apps!

If you dedicate more time to *VIDEO GAMES*
than playing with the kids...

**I'll waste more money on
CELLPHONE APPS than the
Internet bill.**

If you STEAL the remote control batteries again
for who-knows-what...

**I'll CONVERT every appliance to
operate with the Clapper.
Clap. Clap. Clap.**

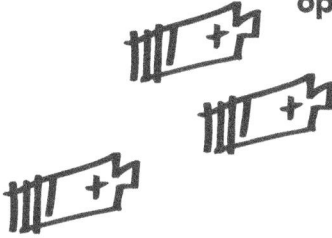

If you CHANGE the TV channel the
moment it gets interesting one more time...

**I'll TALK through the best parts
of the movie.**

If you steal the TOASTY WARM COVERS
while we're sleeping...

**I'll wear those UGLY FLEECE
PAJAMA PANTS that you hate while
we're walking around town.**

If you forget your WALLET on our big night out again...

I'll tighten up the PURSE strings when you want to order the biggest steak in town.

If you forget to bring my sunglasses to the BARBECUE in the park...after I kindly asked three, four, five times...

I'll refill your suntan lotion with RANCH DRESSING and RELISH.

If you're a CRYING RYAN during my high school reunion...

I'll be a DEBBIE DOWNER when it comes to your big birthday celebration.

PUT
YOUR
SHIRT
ON!

**If you make a fool out of yourself
at MY OFFICE PARTY...**

*I'll tell YOUR BOSS the next time
that you play hooky.*

If you transform our garage into the neighborhood FANTASY FOOTBALL HEADQUARTERS...

I'll convert the rest of the house into a BEAUTY BOUTIQUE AND SPA.

If you SELL my dirty beloved college recliner on Craigslist...

I'll DONATE your childhood Barbie Dolls to charity. Yep. Even the pink Corvette and kitchenette set.

If you JAM PACK the bathroom with every possible scent of lotion and soap...

I'll AIR OUT my sports-superstition-never-get-washed socks in the bedroom.
Of course, one pair per league.

If you hang your CHILDHOOD BALLERINA PHOTOS in the bedroom...

I'll display every PEEWEE SPORTS TROPHY I ever won on the living room mantel.

**If you turn into a SILENT MIME
the moment you get upset...**

*I'll try escalating every disagreement into a
SUMO-SIZED SCREAMING MATCH.*

If you always SWEAT THE SMALL STUFF...

*I'll always forget our pursuit of the BIG PICTURE.
You know...like choosing a fancy new boat
instead of a 401k. Or a new set of golf clubs
instead of health insurance.*

*If you're more INDECISIVE than a chameleon traipsing across
a Twister mat...*

**I'll stubbornly WANT MY WAY more than
a mule having a "me" day. NEIGH...
Or whatever sound it is that a mule makes.**

If you COMPLAIN about everything under the sun...

I'll be more HIGH MAINTENANCE than an umbrella in high winds. Really really high winds.

If you ACCIDENTALLY FORGET the last, only, and soon-to-be-needed phone charger on our week-long vacation...

I'll pack MORE STUFF than a department store on our next weekend away.

If you buy my new carry-on luggage bag one size bigger than is AIRLINE ACCEPTABLE.

I'll hide change in all of your pockets before you go through AIRPORT SECURITY. Jingle. Jingle. X-ray Jingle.

If you wear your smelly gym clothes on our ALL-DAY DRIVE one more time...

I'll make us listen to my favorite song 37 TIMES IN A ROW ROW ROW ROW ROW ROW ROW ROW ROW ROW ROW ROW ROW ROW ROW ROW ROW ROW ROW...on our way there.

If you spend our whole VACATION budget on new outfits for the trip...

I'll replace everything in your SUITCASE with Halloween costumes and Christmas sweaters the moment before we leave. Yeah, the ones with the bells. Jing-a-ling-a-ling.

If I return from my work trip to find that you've gone FULL BACHELOR MODE in the house... complete with pizza boxes, beer bottles, and dirty socks everywhere...

I'll "welcome" you home with that NEW SOFA that I've been eyeing.... the next time that you're away.

If you make another meal with LEFTOVERS OF LEFTOVERS OF LEFTOVERS...

I will tell the SAME OL' BAD JOKES again and again while we eat.

What happened when the FROG's car broke down? It got TOAD AWAY!

If you make me accompany you SHOPPING for your underwear...

**I'll ask you to IRON mine.
No starch, please.**

If you FRIEND all of my exes on Facebook...

I'll FOLLOW all of yours on Instagram. #Awesome

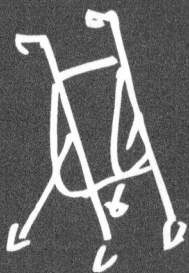

you
drive
me

CraZy!

elsewhere in the world

If you point out my RECEEDING HAIRLINE at the high school reunion...

I'll make sure to remind us all that you've had the SAME HAIRCUT since junior high. High and tight. With a heavy dose of Aqua Net.

If you take PHOTOS OF EVERY DISH that comes to our table...

I'll neglect to point out the SALAD IN YOUR TEETH when it comes to group picture time.

If you arrive for a "workout" dolled up like you're going to the PROM...

I'll pose in the mirror for three sets of selfies like I've been CROWNED THE KING of the gym.

If YOU BADGER ME every 20 minutes until I like your inspirational, motivational, I'm-trying-to-be-a-better-person Facebook posts...

I'll keep sending you ONLINE GAME INVITATIONS until you finally cave to my persistence. Let's play!

If you add a bunch of letters to a word to COVER UP the fact that you don't know how to spellll it...

I'll reply "Haha" to that message when I have NO IDEA what you're talking about. And I don't want to take the time to figure it out.

If you are a PEEPING TOM whenever I look at my phone on the train...

I'll be a CHATTY CATHY by texting my friends about the weirdo next to me. In a jumbo font size. Like a handheld billboard for all the world to see.

mullet →
mullet →
mullet →

ROCKIN'

If you throw yourself another PITY PARTY on social media...

I'll cheer you up with sharing your YOUTHFULLY FOOLISH photos that you hope the world never sees. Mullets galore!

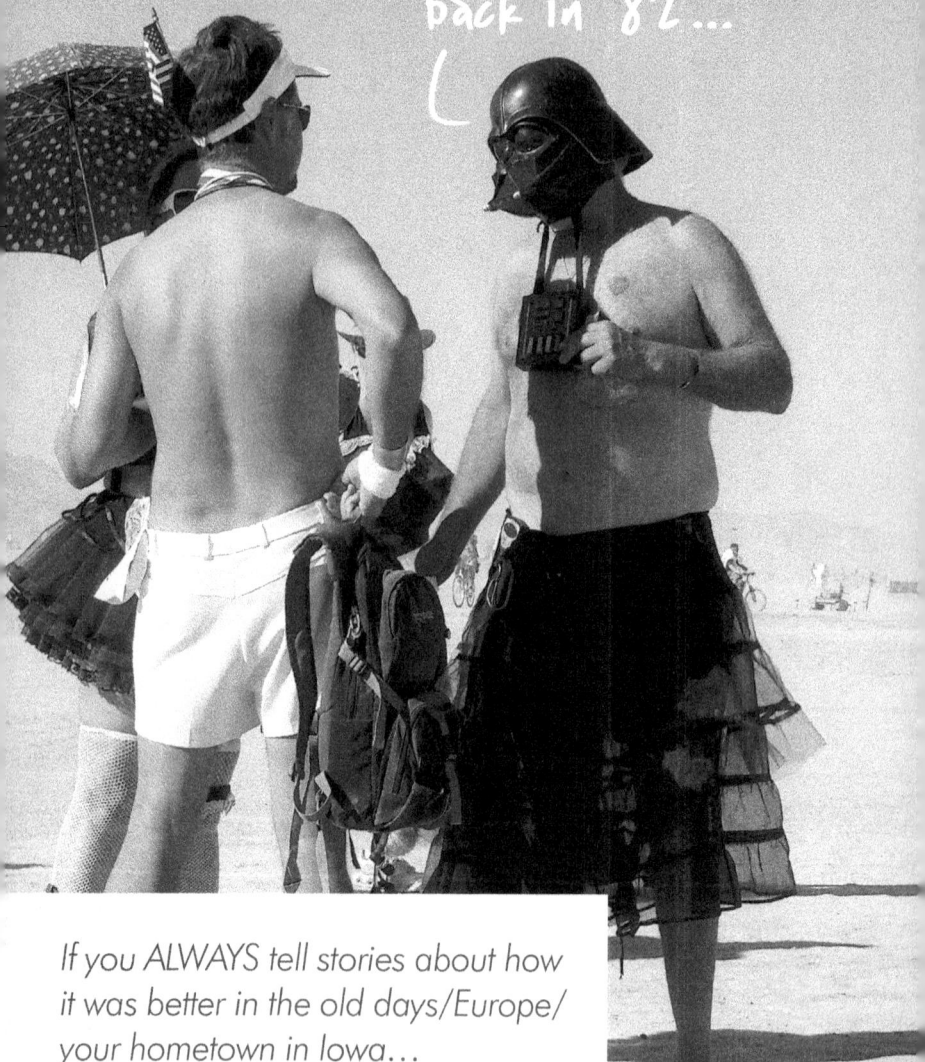

back in '82...

If you ALWAYS tell stories about how
it was better in the old days/Europe/
your hometown in Iowa…

**I'll ONLY tell stories that end with
"Well, I guess you had to be there."
"You would've loved it."**

If you act like you know
EVERYTHING ABOUT EVERYTHING…

I'll pretend like I DON'T REMEMBER that I'm supposed to help you move your couch next weekend. Because I got free tickets to the game. Box seats even. The comfy ones that recline!

If you keep arguing even though you've clearly LOST THE DEBATE…

I'll pretend like I have to go to the bathroom just to CHANGE THE SUBJECT.

If you ask me why I'm still SINGLE…

I'll act surprised when you mention that you have a GIRLFRIEND.

If you TAKE THREE ROUNDS OF DRINKS to decide what you want to order at the restaurant..

I'll SLOPPILY GOBBLE up my dinner the moment our meal arrives. Check please!

If you TEXT YOUR FRIENDS all the way through our highly anticipated dinner...

I'll order an extra meal to take home to EACH OF MY ROOMMATES. You're paying, right?

If you're RUDE to the restaurant servers for no good reason...

I'll suggest that you MAKE NICE with a 50 percent gratuity once the bill comes. Now that's a TIP!

so thirsty!

If you chomp your chips like a HUNGRY HUNGRY HIPPO during lunch...

I'll slurp the last of my soda like I have the world's worst case of DESERT DEHYDRATION.

If you block my concert view with your homemade desperation sign "MARRY ME, DIRTY DRUMMER DUDE"...

I'll sing along so loud that NO ONE CAN HEAR the actual music.

If you LIGHT UP YOUR SKUNK WEED in front of my 12-year-old kid at the outdoor bluegrass concert...

I'll "accidentally" SPILL MY BEER on you to put out the flame. Oops?

If you're three levels TOO LOUD and ROWDY at the ball game...

I'll calm your UNRULINESS by asking to let me pass for my 37TH TRIP to the concession stand. Because corn dogs make me happy. Nachos too.

If, midway through, you blurt out what happens at the END OF THE MOVIE...

I'll put my FEET UP ON THE BACK of your chair as a reminder that you're not the only person here. Maybe I'll even rock your chair a little. Slowly. Gently. In hopes that it lulls you to Zzzzz.

If you keep YAKKING on the phone about your nonsense drama while behind me at the grocery store checkout...

I'll HOLD UP the shopping line ahead of you by running back to grab that one thing I forgot.
Deodorant.
Oh yeah.
And milk too.
Skim, of course.

If you BLOCK the grocery aisle with your shopping cart...

I'll clearly JUDGE everything you have in it until you move out of the way.
Seriously, dude.
Froot Loops are for kids.

If you think that TAKING two and a half parking spaces at the grocery store is okay...

I'll pretend that SURROUNDING your car with three shopping carts is okay too.

If I see you heading to the express lane with your SHOPPING CART PILED HIGH, with obviously more than 10 items or less...

I'll RACE in front of you with my two shopping carts full of stuff. Yeah, two carts. Full.

wanna race?

If you leave your coffee cup on the ground after a dramatically MISSED basketball shot into the trash bin...

I'll pass you back the rebound until you finally MAKE it into the basket.

**If you JINGLE the change in your pocket
every time you're standing still...**

*I'll WHISTLE every time I walk by.
Heigh-ho.
Heigh-ho.
Off to work I go.*

*If you HOP AROUND the sidewalk like
you're avoiding stepping on a crack,
because you know it'll break your momma's back...*

**I'll accidentally BUMP INTO YOU while I walk and
texting to check that mine's having a good day.**

**If you take up half of the sidewalk with your
CIRCUS-TENT-SIZED UMBRELLA...**

*I'll clog up the other half
with my lazy Sunday SLOW STROLL
during the Monday morning commute.*

If you take up the middle of the ESCALATOR
such that we have to monkey climb past you...

I'll stop at the bottom so you can enjoy the log jam of EAGER BEAVERS anxious to get on their way. Because I have to tie my shoe and TWEET while I do it.

If you push your way onto the ELEVATOR as I'm trying to get off...

I'll leave you with a cloud of FLATUALATIONS on my way out. Because my butt is a loaded weapon, always ready to burst into action.

If you DON'T SAY THANK YOU as I hold the door open for you...

I'll let it go in hopes that it hits you ON THE BEHIND on your way through.

If you act like PERSONAL SPACE is a foreign concept...

I'll take BOTH ARMRESTS on the 12-hour flight overseas. Oh. Sorry. My elbow in your ribs doesn't feel good?

If you *TAILGATE* me the entire way home...

I'll drive TOO slowly in the fast lane, TOO fast in the slow lane and CUT YOU OFF on my way to the exit.

If you cruise through every STOP SIGN, RED LIGHT, and TRAFFIC SIGN on your bicycle...

I'll HONK at you the moment you get outside of the bike lane. Safety first!!!

If you BLAB to your friends on speakerphone on the bus...

I'll SPRAWL myself across four seats so that you have nowhere to sit.

Manspreading
+ gym bag
+ briefcase
= I NEED a lot of room.

If you BLARE your car stereo loud enough to rattle everyone's car doors...

I'll HONK my horn every time the stoplight turns green. And toot toot toot to the music. How's my rhythm?

If you decorate your house like the tackiest silly circus FUN HOUSE for every holiday...

I'll plaster the neighborhood with YARD SALE signs for a get-it-now-get-it-cheap celebration at your house.

If you let your dog BARK BARK BARK all night long...

I'll let mine POOOOOOP in your yard. And of course, leave it behind for you to find.

If you fire up your LAWN MOWER at 6 a.m. when I'm trying to sleep in...

I'll leaf-blow MY leaves into YOUR yard this afternoon.

If every evening at your house is a PARTY of bad karaoke and fireworks...

Every early morning at mine will be a revvvvv-v-v-VVVVV-ing good time of working on my motorcycle.

If you HALF-HEARTEDLY APOLOGIZE for your kid running around the store like a wild animal...

I'll WHOLE-HEARTEDLY SUGGEST how you should tame him into domestic acceptability.

If you PRETEND that you can't hear your kid crying...

**I'll ACT like I didn't hear
mine say the S-word.
And the F-word.
B-word too.**

**If you judge my parenting skills by the
NUMBER OF FEATURES my stroller has...**

*I'll judge yours by how many EXCUSES YOU MAKE for
your child's recent temper tantrum.*

"Oh, Little Johnny is tired and constipated?"

*"Oh, Little Johnny gets so restless couped up in his
double-decker stroller with sundeck and mini-fridge."*

*If you BRAG about your kids like they're the world's
future best rocket scientists. And supermodels. And
soccer stars. And singing pop idols.*

**I'll let mine act like suburban gangsters.
SAGGY BAGGY PANTS included.**

If you pee on the SEAT one more time...

*I'll TURN THE BATHROOM LIGHTS OFF the next time
I see your feet under the stall.*

*If you block my way to the sink because you're
FIXING YOUR HAIR for the third time...*

**I'll ask you to move over for my
OH-SO-URGENT-SELFIE in front
of the bathroom mirror.
Smiley face!
Pouty face!
Now with duck lips!**

If you're that LOUD PHONE TALKER in the toilet stall...

**I'll be that CREEPY PHONE TEXTER
at the urinal. So creepy. Ugh. I'm weirding
myself out just thinking about it.**

YARD
SALE!

TOO SMALL T-SHIRT
Title/Date: Vintage Unretouched Photo Of Father And Daughter Watering
Garden / Date not listed
Source: Elzbieta Sekowska (Shutterstock - Image ID: 68447266) http://www.
shutterstock.com/gallery-133975p1.html
Credit/Copyright Attribution: Elzbieta Sekowska/Shutterstock
License: Standard Shutterstock License obtained for usage
Photographer: Unknown.

ACTION AND DRAMA
Title/Date: Tramore Golf Links / 18 September 1907
Source: National Library Of Ireland on The Commons (Flickr)
Credit/Copyright Attribution: Creative Commons. CC0 Public Domain. National
Library Of Ireland on The Commons (Flickr)
License: No known copyrights restrictions.
Photographer: Unknown

GAMES AND APPS
Title/Date: Kiss In Black And White / 19 December 2009
Source: See-Ming Lee (Flickr) https://www.flickr.com/photos/
seeminglee/4211914177/
Credit/Copyright Attribution: See-Ming Lee (Flickr)
License: Creative Commons. Attribution 2.0 Generic (CC BY 2.0).
https://creativecommons.org/licenses/by/2.0/legalcode
Photographer: See-Ming Lee

OFFICE PARTY ORNAMENT
Title/Date: Christmas In Germany / 17 December 2008
Source: Infinite Ache (Flickr) https://www.flickr.com/photos/
infiniteache/5292902766
Credit/Copyright Attribution: Infinite Ache (Flickr)
License: Creative Commons. Attribution 2.0 Generic (CC BY 2.0).
https://creativecommons.org/licenses/by/2.0/legalcode
Photographer: Infinite Ache

FANTASY FOOTBALL BEAUTY BOUTIQUE
Title/Date: San Francisco / 10 September 2014
Source: Karlis Dambrans (Flickr) https://www.flickr.com/photos/
janitors/15608548598
Credit/Copyright Attribution: Karlis Dambrans (Flickr)
License: Creative Commons. Attribution 2.0 Generic (CC BY 2.0).
https://creativecommons.org/licenses/by/2.0/legalcode
Photographer: Karlis Dambrans

HIGH WINDS HAY BALE
Title/Date: Afternoon Hay Bale / 14 June 2014
Source: https://freepixelstock.com/?page=58
Credit/Copyright Attribution: No copyright restrictions. No attribution required.
License: No copyright restrictions. No attribution required.
Photographer: Unknown

YARD SALE!

www.ingramcontent.com/pod-product-compliance
Lightning Source LLC
Chambersburg PA
CBHW072043040426
42447CB00012BB/2986